DONALD GLOVER

THERESE M. SHEA

PowerKiDS
press.™

New York

Published in 2022 by The Rosen Publishing Group, Inc.
29 East 21st Street, New York, NY 10010

Copyright © 2022 by The Rosen Publishing Group, Inc.

First Edition

Editor: Greg Roza
Designer: Rachel Rising

Photo Credits: Cover, pp. 1, 7 VALERIE MACON/Contributor/AFP; pp. 4, 6, 8, 10, 12, 14, 16, 18, 20, 21 Woskresenskiy/shutterstock.com; pp. 4, 6, 8, 10, 12, 14, 16, 18, 20, 21 Sunward Art/shutterstock.com; p. 5 Mike Coppola/MG18/Contributor/Getty Images Entertainment; p. 9 Michael Kovac/Contributor/WireImage/ Getty Images; p. 11 Jason LaVeris/Contributor/FilmMagic/Getty Images; p. 13 Stefanie Keenan/Contributor/ Getty Images Entertainment/Getty Images; p. 15 Steve Granitz/Contributor/WireImages/Getty Images; p. 17 Bryan Bedder/Stringer/Getty Images Entertainment/Getty Images; p. 19 Alberto E. Rodriguez/Stringer/Getty Images Entertainment/Getty Images; p. 21 Monica Schipper/Contributor/WireImages/Getty Images.

Library of Congress Cataloging-in-Publication Data

Names: Shea, Therese, author.
Title: Donald Glover / Therese M. Shea.
Description: New York : PowerKids Press, [2022] | Series: African American
    superstars | Includes index.
Identifiers: LCCN 2020039416 | ISBN 9781725326071 (library binding) | ISBN
    9781725326057 (paperback) | ISBN 9781725326064 (6 pack)
Subjects: LCSH: Glover, Donald, 1983–Juvenile literature. | African
    American entertainers–Biography–Juvenile literature. | African
    American singers–Biography–Juvenile literature.
Classification: LCC PN2287.G556 S54 2022 | DDC 782.421649092 [B]–dc23
LC record available at https://lccn.loc.gov/2020039416

Manufactured in the United States of America

CPSIA Compliance Information: Batch #CSPK22. For Further Information contact Rosen Publishing, New York, New York at 1-800-237-9932.

Find us on

CONTENTS

Many Talents

Donald Glover is an actor, writer, and director. He created his own TV show. He's also a rapper. Glover has many **creative** ideas. He began with jobs in **comedy**. However, his work takes on serious problems like **racism** too.

Family Life

Donald McKinley Glover was born September 25, 1983, in California. His family moved near Atlanta, Georgia. His parents **fostered** many children. They **adopted** two. Donald also has another brother and sister. He often works with his brother Stephen.

Creative Kid

In high school, Glover acted in plays. He decided to go to New York University Tisch School of the Arts. He studied writing there. He was also interested in comedy. In 2006, he began writing for the TV show *30 Rock*.

Community

Glover worked for *30 Rock* for three years. He learned about writing for TV and working with actors and crew. In 2009, he got a role, or part, on the show *Community*. He played an ex-football player named Troy.

MEDIA

PALEY CENTE

Childish Gambino

Glover uses the name Childish Gambino when he raps. His music talks about being a Black man in America. He received his first Grammy Award in 2018. In 2019, he won four Grammys for the song "This Is America."

Atlanta

Glover **developed** the TV show *Atlanta*. It's about the lives of several Black men. In 2017, Glover became the first African American to win an Emmy Award for best director of a comedy. He won best actor too.

Lando

In 2018, Glover played Lando Calrissian in the movie *Solo: A Star Wars Story*. Glover grew up watching Star Wars movies. He loved playing Lando. Many people wanted him to have his own *Star Wars* movie.

Simba

In 2019, Disney created a remake of the movie *The Lion King*. Glover was the voice of Simba, the young lion prince. Glover's father died while the movie was being made. He said this loss helped him play the character.

19

More to Come

Childish Gambino made new music in 2020. Glover plans to stop making music. He won't stop his many other creative plans. He helps a **charity** for foster and adopted children. Glover's fans can't wait to see what he does next!

TIMELINE

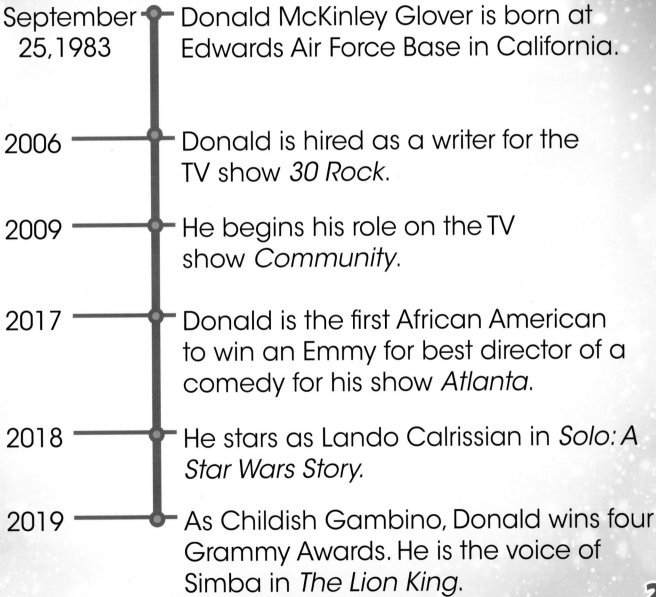

September 25, 1983 — Donald McKinley Glover is born at Edwards Air Force Base in California.

2006 — Donald is hired as a writer for the TV show *30 Rock*.

2009 — He begins his role on the TV show *Community*.

2017 — Donald is the first African American to win an Emmy for best director of a comedy for his show *Atlanta*.

2018 — He stars as Lando Calrissian in *Solo: A Star Wars Story.*

2019 — As Childish Gambino, Donald wins four Grammy Awards. He is the voice of Simba in *The Lion King*.

GLOSSARY

adopt: To make part of a family.

charity: An organization that helps people or animals.

comedy: A movie, play, book, or performance meant to make people laugh.

creative: Being able to make new things or think of new ideas.

develop: To create over time.

foster: To give parental care to a child who isn't adopted or related to you.

racism: The belief that one group or race of people is better than another group or race.

FOR MORE INFORMATION

BOOKS

Ireland, Justina. *Star Wars: Lando's Luck*. San Francisco, CA: Disney Lucasfilm Press, 2018.

Norris, Hayley. *Donald Glover*. New York, NY: Enslow, 2020.

WEBSITES

Donald Glover
www.imdb.com/name/nm2255973
Read more about Glover's acting career.

Donald Glover Biography
www.biography.com/actor/donald-glover
Learn more about Glover's life and career here.

INDEX

A
awards, 12, 14, 21

C
Childish Gambino, 12, 20, 21
comedy, 4, 8, 14, 21

D
director, 4, 14, 21

F
family, 6, 18

M
movies, 16, 18

R
rapper, 4, 12

S
school, 8

T
TV shows, 4, 8, 10, 14, 21